W0323946

Fanny Harper

Glasgow Meets Edinburgh

Access all the accompanying digital components for this book on **allango**, the DELTA Publishing language learning platform:

Scan the QR code or go directly to **www.allango.co.uk**	Search for the title or the ISBN and click on the cover image	Access content, use now or save for later

When you see this symbol, accompanying digital content is available.

DELTA Publishing

Images:
4.1 123RF.com (jennifersophie), Nidderau; **4.2** 123RF.com (naumoid); **5.1** 123RF.com (alexeyfedoren); **5.2** 123RF.com (liudmilachernetska); **5.3** 123RF.com (ruslankphoto); **5.4** 123RF.com (deyandenchev); **5.5** 123RF.com (foodandmore); **5.6** 123RF.com (lukassek); **5.7** 123RF.com (moravia); **89** 123RF.com (liorpt)

Text credits:
pp. 34-35 William Shakespeare, The Merchant of Venice, 1596-97

1st edition 1 5 4 3 2 1 | 2028 27 26 25 24

Delta Publishing, 2024
www.deltapublishing.co.uk

Author: Fanny Harper
Editor: Kate Baade
Cover and layout: Andreas Drabarek, Eva Lettenmayer
Illustrations: Szilvia Szakall, Beehive Illustration
Design: Datagroup int, Timisoara
Cover picture: Szilvia Szakall, Beehive Illustration
Printing and binding: Plump Druck & Medien GmbH; Rheinbreitbach

Printed in Germany
ISBN 978-3-12-501173-1

PEFC
Förderung nachhaltiger Waldbewirtschaftung
PEFC/04-31-3752
www.pefc.de

Contents

Abbreviations

sb somebody
sth something

Before you start

Scotland is famous for the following things. Match the words with the pictures.

a. porridge	b. haggis	c. tartan	d. loch	e. bagpipes	f. kilts

1. 
2. 
3. 
4. 
5. 
6. 

1	2	3	4	5	6
c	a	d	f	b	e.

Scotland is one of the countries of the United Kingdom. Can you name the others?
Put the countries in the box and add as much information as you can for each country.

country	Scotland		
cities		Belfast Nottingham	
flag colours			red / green / white
symbols			leek / daffodil
famous things	Nessie		
famous people		Robin Hood	

How do you think Scotland is different from the other countries in the United Kingdom? And from the country you live in?

Chapter 1

"Do you have to wear *that*?"

Jessie had made a long skirt from two pairs of jeans and put a peace and love sign on the back pocket. Jessie was pleased with her creation, but her mum was not impressed.

"I made it myself," Jessie mumbled. "It's called 'upcycling' because instead of throwing something away, you turn it into something better."

"That is *not* part of the school uniform!" said Mum, as Jessie sat down at the table. She looked at the bowl of grey porridge. Why did her mum always say negative things?

Jessie's mother always made porridge the traditional Scottish way, with water and salt. No milk, no sugar. She said it was healthy. In fact, Jessie's mother was always on a diet. She clearly wanted Jessie to be slim too, but Jessie preferred sweet, milky

22 **impressed** feeling or showing admiration – 29 **porridge** a typical Scottish breakfast of oats boiled in water or milk – 29 **traditional** the usual way of doing things

porridge for breakfast. Well, at least the salty porridge was warm. It was early summer, but Edinburgh was pretty cold. Jessie put a spoonful of porridge in her mouth. It was so hot that her eyes watered.

"You're not *crying* are you?"

"No, of course not!"

"Because when you cry, your face goes red, and your hair looks brighter."

This was not a nice thing to say, but Jessie knew that her mother was only angry with Dad.

Jessie had very red, curly hair, just like her father. Dad had left a year ago, and now Mum was angry all the time. She seemed to think Jessie was responsible – was it because she looked like Dad? Sometimes she told her to dress in a different way, sometimes she told her to lose weight, but she could not tell her to change her hair.

"Well, I'm off to work now. I left twenty pounds on the side. Can you do some shopping after school?"

Jessie waited until her mum shut the door and wondered if she should change her skirt. The uniform was not very strict at her school, but they had to wear a dark blue skirt or trousers, a navy blue jumper, and a red and green tartan tie. Mum was right, she was going to get into trouble wearing that skirt.... but getting into trouble felt exciting. Maybe she should wear the skirt and not go to school? She could go and buy something nice to eat and sit and read her book in the park. Then she could wear her skirt all day.

Jessie used to be a good student, but lately she was fed up. Fed up of school, fed up of Edinburgh, fed up of being told what to do. Mostly, Jessie wanted to stay in bed and read books. She liked crime stories and thrillers, and of course Harry Potter, but in fact

4 **to water** when your eyes fill with tears – 14 **to tell sb to do sth** to order or advise sb – 15 **weight** how heavy sth is – 22 **tartan** a patterned Scottish cloth – 23 **to get into trouble** to be punished for doing sth wrong – 27 **fed up** bored or annoyed – 30 **thriller** an exciting story, often involving crime

she liked all kinds of books, even the ones they had to study at school. She loved the way the words made her feel. At school, it was not cool to like books, so Jessie pretended that she preferred to scroll down her phone like everyone else. It was easier that way.

Jessie put on her coat. It was best to cover your uniform in this part of Edinburgh. She even kept her school tie in her pocket and put it on when she got to the gate. The kids from the other secondary school were bullies and could give you trouble, everyone knew that.

The journey to school always made Jessie feel good. She took the bus along Princess Street, with its souvenir shops down one side and views of Edinburgh Castle on the other side. Sometimes, she saw a piper playing in the street dressed in a kilt and with a hat on the ground for coins. She then walked up to the North Bridge by foot and walked down part of the Royal Mile. Every Edinburgh schoolchild knows that the Royal Mile is actually longer than a mile and that kings and queens used to cross it, but Jessie liked it because of the very old buildings and the brightly coloured shops and pubs. And St Giles Cathedral was pretty impressive too. Sometimes she walked so slowly along the street that she was late for school. Like this morning.

Lately, Jessie had been skipping some of her lessons. She enjoyed finding different ways to avoid classes. Sometimes she just walked out of school in the middle of the day, and no one noticed. She would go to town, buy herself a portion of chips with salt and sauce, and read a book on a park bench, or play games on her phone. Twice she had missed a whole day and then produced a fake letter from her mum saying she had been sick. It was incredibly easy. Another time she said she had missed the

---

3 **to pretend** to act as if sth is true when you know it is not – 4 **to scroll down** to move down the screen – 9 **bully** sb who tries to harm or frighten another person – 14 **piper** sb who plays Scottish bagpipes – 14 **kilt** a Scottish tartan skirt for men – 23 **to skip** to miss / not go – 26 **portion** an amount of food – 29 **fake** not real

bus, but her English teacher, Mr Jones, did not seem to believe her, she could tell by the look in his eye. English had always been her best subject and she had loved it. Until recently.

Unfortunately, Jessie was still too young to leave school and become a clothes designer. She had posted pictures of some of the clothes and bags she had made on social media, but she had not had many 'likes'. As she went to school, she thought she should have put on her school trousers instead of the homemade skirt. She looked at her reflection in a shop window. Her red hair was wild today and she decided that she looked ugly in her skirt. But it was too late to change now. The headmaster, Mr Murray, was at the gate checking everyone's uniform. Oh no! Jessie pulled her coat closer and walked into school very fast.

How does Jessie like to eat her porridge for breakfast?

What are some of the places in Edinburgh she walks past on her way to school?

Think about it...

Jessie has been making upcycled clothes. What do you think about upcycling? What kinds of things can be upcycled apart from clothes?

In the UK, school children have to wear a uniform. Do you think uniforms are a good idea? What are the advantages and the disadvantages?

5 **to post sth** to put sth online – 8 **homemade** made by yourself – 9 **reflection** an image that comes from a mirror

Chapter 2

"We have a new pupil in our class today, everyone. His name is Ian and he has just moved here. It's not easy changing schools in the middle of term, so I'd like you all to make him feel welcome."

The form teacher, Ms Campbell, was a tall woman with a face like a mouse. She looked too old to be a teacher with her tartan skirts, her grey hair and her round glasses. She was like Professor McGonagall in the Harry Potter films, but less impressive. Most of the students carried on talking to each other, but Ms Campbell continued with her introduction.

"Please stand, Ian," she said, giving him a little smile.

A tall, slim boy stood up. He had thick black hair and green eyes, and a long scar down his left cheek. Ian looked at the whole class very slowly and calmly, as if he was trying to find someone, and then his eyes stopped on Jessie. He did not seem very friendly. Jessie looked away quickly. She felt uncomfortable and her face was hot.

"Where were you at school before, Ian?" asked Ms Campbell with a smile.

"*Whit*?" said Ian, rudely.

With just one word, everyone know that Ian was from Glasgow, not from Edinburgh, because of his strong accent. A couple of pupils giggled. "*A weegie!*" whispered someone. Ian glared at the class. He looked very angry. In fact, he looked scary.

The teacher repeated the question, but more slowly.

"I'm from Glasgow. The best."

Now he was looking hard at all the students. His green eyes were burning with anger. No one said anything this time.

That morning, during the maths lesson, Jessie was staring at the blackboard, thinking about how she could transform a check shirt into a bag. Suddenly, she felt something tap the back of her chair. The tapping did not stop. She turned around and saw that Ian was sitting behind her. He was staring hard and his eyes were full of hatred. Why did he hate her? Jessie felt hot and worried. She turned back to the board, but the tapping on the chair continued. Jessie was nervous and unhappy but she did not know what to do. Who was this new Glaswegian boy so full of anger? She decided not to go to maths again.

At break time, most of Jessie's friends were bent over their screens so that the teachers could not see them. This was because your phone was supposed to be turned off during the school day. Of course, nobody turned off their phone. Jessie was interested in some things on social media, like upcycled clothes, but she preferred reading. Hidden by the trees in the corner of the school yard, she was leaning against a tree trunk, absorbed in a book called *The Catcher in the Rye*.

"Hey, carrot top!" someone hissed like a snake. "You are *sooo* ginger my eyes hurt! With your horrible white skin and your orange hair, you look like a traffic cone. "

---

1 **whit** the Scottish pronunciation of "what" – 4 **Weegie** slang for sb from Glasgow – 4 **to glare** to look in a long, angry way – 10 **to stare** to look for a long time with your eyes wide open – 11 **check** fabric pattern with small squares – 15 **hatred** intense dislike – 18 **Glaswegian** from Glasgow – 26 **to be absorbed** to focus your attention – 29 **ginger** red hair, usually negative

The strong Glaswegian accent was easy to recognise. Jessie shut her book and looked up. Ian was looking down at her and he was angry again. Jessie's head was at the level of his tracksuit bottoms, and she could see they were a well-known brand. He gave her a little kick with one of his expensive trainers. She wanted to say something back, but what could she say to this confident Glasgow boy? He was so angry, it was frightening.

He suddenly bent down and whispered in her ear: "Your hooter is enormous! It takes up all of your face." She could feel the heat of his breath against her cheek. Jessie's stomach hurt and she felt dizzy.

In a second, Ian had gone. Jessie put down her book and saw the title was blurred. She wiped her eyes. This time she *was* crying.

How does everyone know that Ian is from Glasgow?

because he had an accent

Where does Jessie go to read during breaktimes?

In the corner of the school yard

Think about it...

Ian thinks that people from Glasgow are better than people from Edinburgh. Have you ever come across that kind of attitude in your country? Where do you think this kind of rivalry comes from?

Ian uses words to make Jessie feel ugly and bad. This is one kind of bullying. What other kinds of bullying exist? Have you ever come across bullying at your school?

3 **tracksuit** sports clothes – 4 **brand** mark of a product – 5 **to kick** to hit with the foot – 5 **trainers** sports shoes – 8 **hooter** slang for nose – 10 **dizzy** when your head seems to turn around – 12 **blurred** not clear – 12 **to wipe** to dry with a cloth or your hand

Chapter 3

Jessie decided not to go to her English lesson after the break. She did not want to see Ian and his angry eyes, so she simply walked out of school and into town. One of the best things about Edinburgh is the hills, the views are amazing. Jessie made her way to Calton Hill and climbed up to the National Monument, which looks like an unfinished Greek temple. She sat on the grass and watched the tourists taking pictures of the building. From up here, Jessie could see Edinburgh Castle and the Balmoral Clock Tower. The city looked ancient and wonderful and Jessie decided that Edinburgh was a beautiful place to live after all. Much better than Glasgow, anyway. Jessie had been to Glasgow twice to see her dad, who had moved there. The city was big and busy and not very pretty. True, her father had taken her to the Willow Tea Rooms designed by Rennie Macintosh, a Scot famous for his Art

30 **busy** full of people – 32 **Scot** sb from Scotland

Nouveau designs. She remembered the funny black chairs with their long backs and the stained-glass windows. But Glasgow did not have anything like the Palace of Holyroodhouse or Edinburgh Castle, or the amazing views. All the tourists came here to visit the monuments. Edinburgh was definitely better.

Later that afternoon, Jessie nearly jumped out of her skin when she saw Mr Jones waiting at the end of her street. She recognised him from a distance because of his bald head, dark beard and glasses. What was her English teacher doing there, and how did he know where she lived?

"Sorry to frighten you, Jessie," he said kindly. "I'm worried that you haven't been coming to English lessons for a while."

Oh no, she was in trouble now! If Mum found out she'd been missing school, she would not be happy. Top grades were almost as important to her mum as thin legs and a flat stomach.

"Don't worry, I'm not going to report you. Not now, anyway. I wanted to know if everything was alright. You are one of the best students, Jessie, maybe the best, and it's a shame to see you waste your talent."

"Well, I do like English, it's just..."

Mr Jones looked down and saw the copy of *The Catcher in the Rye* in Jessie's hands.

"I hope you don't want to get expelled from school, like Holden!" said Mr Jones, referring to the hero of the book.

"No, of course not, it's just..."

Jessie did not really know what to say or where to start. Was it a good idea to tell him about Ian? Or about her mum? Were teachers there to give support, or was their only job to tell you about Shakespeare and maybe J. D. Salinger (the author of *The Catcher in the Rye*)?

---

2 **stained glass** coloured glass – 6 **to jump out of your skin** to be very surprised – 8 **bald** with no hair – 16 **to report** to officially complain – 18 **a shame** unfortunate, regrettable – 19 **talent** natural skill – 23 **to expel** to make sb officially leave school

"Jessie, I wanted to ask you if you'll come to a new poetry club I've started on Thursday lunchbreaks in room 201."

"I really don't think…"

"It's mostly students a bit older than you, and they are all really interested in writing. I think you would enjoy the club. You're a very good writer, I've seen what you can do. And we're having a competition."

"I don't know if…"

"Come on, Jessie, you know you would have fun, I can see you're interested."

"Oh… alright then." It was difficult to say no. And anyway, Jessie felt a flash of excitement. And in fact, she was interested. Usually, she loved writing poetry, although lately she had stopped.

"Great, see you on Thursday at lunchbreak. I have to go now. But you know I'm there if you need me, and so are the other teachers, okay?"

Mr Jones gave her a long, hard look, and it was very different from the long, hard look that Ian had given her that morning. Instead of making her feel ginger and ugly, Mr Jones really seemed to care. He had even said that she was "maybe the best" at English. For the first time for ages, Jessie felt pretty good. She decided that she would go to the poetry club, and that she would return to her English lessons at school.

Which building in Edinburgh looks like an unfinished Greek temple?

Why is Jessie excited about joining the poetry club?

12 **flash** a sudden feeling – 21 **to care** to feel concern or interest

Think about it …

Jessie admires the monuments in her city, Edinburgh. How do you feel about the place you live? Do you find it beautiful?

Jessie has been missing some of her lessons. What would happen to someone in your school if they kept skipping class?

Chapter 4

The next day started off alright. Mum left for work early and Jessie made herself a hot chocolate for breakfast. Geography and biology went okay, in fact they were quite interesting, and she hung out with Margie and Bella during break time. They were sharing Bella's packet of crisps.

"I really like your bag," said Margie.

"I made it from an old shirt."

"No! Did you really?" The girls seemed genuinely impressed.

At that point, she saw Ian walking towards them. Jessie felt her stomach drop like a falling brick.

As he passed by, he stopped suddenly in front of Jessie. He seemed very tall and his green eyes were bright and furious. "Hey, your hair is so bright, I thought you were a stop light, *ginger minger*."

22 **to hang out** to spend time with – 23 **crisps** in the UK, very thin fried potatoes eaten as a snack – 31 **ginger minger** an insult to people with red hair

Jessie's mouth went dry and she was unable to speak. Margie and Bella were looking at her with their mouths open.

Ian pulled up his hood. He was wearing a cool, expensive jacket and he wanted them to see it. He smiled. "You Edinburgh girls are just so ugly," he hissed and walked away slowly.

"Did he really just say that, or did I imagine it?" said Margie.

"Gorgeous guys like Ian think they can get away with anything," said Bella.

"He thinks he's cool because he comes from Glasgow, but he is in the minority here," said Margie. "Glasgow is full of uneducated people who don't speak proper English. All they care about is football, not culture. My mum told me so. Just ignore him, Jessie, your red hair is amazing."

But Jessie did not feel amazing. In fact, she felt sick. She went to sit on her own and tried to read her book, but the words were dancing on the page. She decided not to go to classes that afternoon.

What are the names of Jessie's friends?

What does Ian look like – can you describe him?

Think about it…

Margie says that people from Glasgow are uneducated and don't speak proper English. Where do you think she gets that idea from?

Jessie's friends are there when Ian bullies Jessie. Do you think that they give her enough support? What would you do in that situation? Would you tell a teacher?

3 **hood** a cover for your head that is part of a jacket or coat – 7 **gorgeous** lovely, beautiful – 7 **to get away with** to do sth without punishment – 10 **minority** the smaller part – 12 **to ignore** to not pay attention

Chapter 5

When Thursday came, Jessie spent the whole morning worrying about whether to go to poetry club or not. She imagined everyone turning to stare at her when she walked in the room, whispering, "Who's that new ginger girl? Look at her ridiculous clothes!"

She decided not to go, and was about to go off towards the trees to read her new book, *Trainspotting* by Irvine Welsh, when she found herself face to face with Mr Jones in the corridor!

"Oh, Jessie, I'm so glad you're coming to poetry club. Come with me, room 201 is just over there."

It really felt as if Mr Jones had been waiting for her, but there was not much she could do about it now. Slowly, she followed him into the room. About ten people were already sitting in a circle of chairs. She recognised some of them from around

22 **to whisper** to talk very quietly – 26 **corridor** a passage in a building

school, but they were all a bit older than her. Everyone looked up and smiled. They seemed to smile right into her eyes.

"This is Jessie," said Mr Jones, who was standing right behind her. "The brilliant English student I told you about."

Jessie felt her face go hot. She was sure that she looked like a purple beetroot. *A purple face and orange hair, I must look terrible*, she thought.

"Hey there, Jessie, welcome!" said someone, and then everyone else joined in: "Hi Jessie, great to have you here." "Come and sit down." An electric thrill shot through Jessie's body. She felt important.

And so she sat down, and Mr Jones started to talk about writing poetry, about opening up your emotions, turning them into words, and putting them on the page. He told them about characters and metaphors and about listening to your thoughts. Instead of worrying about how she looked and gazing out the window, Jessie was totally absorbed by what Mr Jones was saying. She felt inspired. At the end of the session Mr Jones read them a poem called *In Mrs Tilscher's Class* by Carol Ann Duffy, and it was amazing. Then he told them to write their own poem. He said he was going to choose one of the poems for a special reading. As soon as Jessie started writing, the words ran from her pen with a life of their own.

As she handed in her paper and turned to leave, a girl put her hand on Jessie's shoulder.

"Your skirt is absolutely amazing. Did you make it yourself?" It was a girl called Siri.

"Um, yes, I did, from a couple of pairs of jeans."

Two other students, Zara and Elliot, had come closer too. "You are so talented!" gasped Elliot.

"I would like to order one," said Siri. "How much do you sell them for?"

---

6 **beetroot** a purple root vegetable – 9 **to join in** to do sth together – 18 **to be inspired** to be filled with ideas – 31 **to order** to ask for sth to be supplied/made

"Me too," Zara joined in. "What other kinds of clothes do you make?"

Before she knew it, Jessie had agreed to meet up with the others after school in the coffee shop over the road. She felt like a balloon full of air, ready to float high in the sky. It was a wonderful feeling.

What book is Jessie reading now?

Why does Siri admire Jessie during the poetry club?

Think about it ...

The poetry club starts to build up Jessie's confidence because writing is something she can do well. What kind of clubs would you like to see at your school?

5 **to float** to move slowly in the air

Chapter 6

The coffee shop was a popular student hang-out but Jessie had never been there before. She was nervous, and felt sure that everyone would turn and stare at her when she opened the door. She thought they would all be slim and attractive.

The place was very busy, and no one even looked up when she opened the door. Jessie couldn't see Elliot, Zara and Siri, and she felt so nervous that she decided to go home after all.

"Hey, Jessie, over here!" came a voice, and she saw them waving at her energetically from a table in the corner.

They made space for her and immediately started asking her about her sewing.

"Where did you get all of your ideas from?" asked Elliot.

"Who taught you to sew like that?" said Siri.

26 **to wave** to move your hand as a signal – 29 **to sew** to make clothes or anything from cloth

"I really want to buy a skirt from you. How much do you sell them for?" asked Zara.

"You should get a stall in Stockbridge Market. My sister sells handmade soap there and she loves it."

"Do you think anyone would be interested…?"

"You're joking, of *course* they would!"

They were all so positive that once again, Jessie started to feel better about herself.

"Stand up and let me have another look at that skirt," said Zara. "You look so good in that!"

"Oh, I don't know about that…" she began.

"What do you mean?"

"Well, my mother said it made me look fat."

"Oh not another toxic mum!" groaned Siri. "My mother's always telling me that I dress really badly and how she hates my piercings."

"Yeah, me too," added Zara. "My mum wants me to cover up every centimetre of my body in really baggy clothes. But that's her problem. Really, Jessie, your skirt is amazing and you look beautiful in it."

Beautiful? Jessie felt herself go red.

"You look like a woman from a Rubens painting," said Elliot.

"A what painting?"

"Rubens was one of the Dutch masters. He loved to paint plump women with lots of soft skin. Back then, in the 17th century, thin was considered ugly."

"But I'm ginger and I have a big nose and white skin…"

"What do you mean by that?" said Elliot. "All the best Scottish women have red hair. Look at Mary Queen of Scots."

"Really?"

"*Aye*, she had red hair, a long nose and white skin, and look how powerful she was."

3 **stall** a stand in a market – 14 **toxic** unpleasant, bad for you – 14 **to groan** to make a deep sound to show emotion – 17 **baggy** loose, not tight – 24 **plump** round and full – 30 **aye** Scottish for 'yes'

"But that was in the sixteenth century..."

"Don't you see, Jessie, it's all about fashion," said Zara. "Just be yourself, Jessie. You write beautiful poems, you make creative clothes, you have the most beautiful red hair and skin like porcelain."

"Porcelain?" mumbled Jessie. "But people laugh at me..."

"Forget your mum, she's just jealous. She needs to get a life of her own..."

"No, I think I can deal with my mum. But there's this new boy called Ian..."

And so Jessie told them about the bullying. Zara, Elliot and Siri listened to her carefully. When she had finished, Zara said, "You *have* to report it. Tell your form teacher. Or tell Mr Jones, he's a really cool teacher, he would sort it out for you."

"*Aye*. But I don't know. Maybe I can deal with it..."

"Look," said Siri, putting her hand on Jessie's shoulder, "people who bully always have no confidence. This boy Ian must be feeling bad about something in his own life. You say he's from Glasgow, and you know how much rivalry there is between Glasgow and Edinburgh. He probably hates living here. Or perhaps he feels bad because Edinburgh is so beautiful, and Glasgow is so industrial and Glaswegians have such a strong accent and they eat terrible food..."

"Siri!" shouted Elliot. "You're not being very open-minded!"

"Well, that's true. But you know, this Ian is probably feeling lonely and different in Edinburgh. Whereas you are in your home town. And don't forget, you are *also* really talented!"

5 **porcelain** fine white ceramic – 7 **jealous** feeling unhappy that someone has / does something better – 9 **to deal with** to know what to do with – 14 **to sort out** to find a solution – 19 **rivalry** competition to be the best – 22 **industrial** full of factories – 24 **open-minded** acceptance of differences – 26 **lonely** sad to have no friends

Elliot compares Jessie to the paintings of which famous painter?

Which Scottish queen does he mention?

Think about it …

Siri talks about “toxic” mums who want their children to look a particular way. Do you think that parents should let their children wear what they want? What about piercings and tattoos?

Siri, Elliot and Zara think that Ian probably feels lonely after moving to a new town and that is why he is being a bully. Do you think that schools should support new students, perhaps by asking someone to be their special friend (a “buddy”)?

Chapter 7

After the poetry club, Jessie decided to go back to English class. English was definitely her favourite subject, but for some reason, it was the class she skipped the most.

When she arrived in the room, Ian was already sitting at a desk at the back of the class. He looked at her slowly and shook his head as if to say, "Oh dear, you are so ugly." Jessie's face became very hot and her heart started racing. She went to sit next to Bella at the front of the classroom.

Mr Jones came in the room and started the lesson. They were studying *The Merchant of Venice* by Shakespeare and today they were talking about Shylock. In Shakespeare's story, Shylock is a money lender, and he is treated badly because he is a Jew. Mr Jones said that in Elizabethan times, when Shakespeare wrote the play, Shylock would have been seen as a villain.

"What do you think about Shylock? Is he a bad guy or a good guy?" he asked the class.

23 **to race** to go very fast – 28 **to lend** to let so use sth, but you have to give it back – 29 **Elizabethan times** when Elizabeth I was queen (1558-1603) – 30 **villain** a bad guy

"He's a victim!" said John. "He's clearly being bullied simply because he's a Jew!"

"Do you all think that?" said Mr Jones, looking round the class.

"Yes, I agree," said Lily. "Antonio even kicks him and calls him names. That's classic bullying!"

"Very interesting," said Mr Jones, clearly enjoying the discussion. "So, can we find evidence of this in Shakespeare's text?" He looked towards the back of the classroom and frowned. "Ian, what are you doing? What are you doing to Julia? From here, it looks as if you're kicking the back of her chair."

The whole class turned round to look at Ian, who stared back at Mr Jones. "No, I wasn't doing anything." His voice was very sure and calm.

"Is that true, Julia?" asked Mr Jones.

Julia looked down at her desk and mumbled that it was true. Mr Jones frowned again.

"Well, Ian. Perhaps you can read a bit of Shakespeare for us now. Page 57. Start from, '*I am a Jew*', then keep reading, please."

He looked down at his own copy of the play, waiting for Ian to begin.

Nothing.

Mr Jones looked up again. "Can't you find the page, Ian? When you are ready, please start with, '*I am a Jew. Hath not a Jew eyes*?'"

The whole class turned towards the back of the class, and watched Ian. Even Jessie looked round and saw that Ian had gone bright red. He was staring at his paper with horror as if he had just discovered a dead body. And he still said nothing.

"Ian?"

"*I am a Jew.... Tha..... Ha...?*" He looked up at Mr Jones for help. His eyes were shining with panic. For the first time, Ian did

1 **victim** sb who suffers as a result of sb else – 7 **evidence** sth that shows sth is true – 8 **frown** a facial expression showing that you are not happy – 18 **'I am a Jew'** Shakespeare's 'I am a Jew' speech from *The Merchant of Venice* is very famous, because it challenges racist attitudes. The clear message of the speech: we are all the same and we need to treat everyone equally and fairly – 19 **play** story acted at the theatre – 30 **panic** uncontrollable fear

not look confident. In fact, he looked frightened. Frightened of what? Of words?

"Yes, 'hath' is old English. It just means 'have'. In modern English, 'hath not a Jew eyes' means something like, 'doesn't a Jew have eyes?'. Carry on from there, please." Mr Jones voice was slow and encouraging.

Ian stammered as he tried the next sentence. "*Hath.. not a … Jew … hands, gorn.. min…*"

He came to a stop and raised his eyes miserably, like a dog that has done something wrong. "I can't do it," he stammered and his voice was very small.

Nobody said anything. Total silence. The whole class had turned their heads to look at Ian.

"I… I'm dyslexic. It's… quite bad." Ian fixed a point on the wall and looked at it angrily. The same kind of anger as when he looked at Jessie.

Mr Jones immediately started talking in his soft, calm voice. "I'm sorry, Ian, I had no idea. Normally, the school should know about this, the information should be in your school file. Come and see me after class, please, and we'll organise some support for you. We are there to help, remember that."

Mr Jones was smiling kindly but Ian had gone very white. He was clearly embarrassed. He wasn't looking at anyone anymore, he was only looking at his desk.

"Now… Jessie, could you please read the next few lines?" asked Mr Jones.

"*I am a Jew. Hath not a Jew eyes? Hath not a Jew hands, organs, dimensions, senses, affections, passions? Fed with the same food, hurt with the same weapons, subject to the same diseases, healed by the same means, warmed and cooled by the same winter and summer, as a Christian is? If you prick us, do we not bleed? If you tickle us, do we not laugh? If you poison us, do we not die?*"

---

6 **to encourage** to give support – 7 **to stammer** to stop and repeat words without wanting to – 14 **dyslexia** learning difficulty mainly involving reading

"And what does that mean, Jessie? Can you say that in simple English?"

"It means that we are all the same. We are all humans and we all deserve to be treated the same."

Jessie did not look at Ian as she left the classroom.

"That horrible Glaswegian bully turns out to be really thick!" laughed Bella as they walked out the door.

That evening, Jessie looked up 'dyslexia' on her computer. She discovered that there were several types of dyslexics. Some people saw the letters in the wrong order. For others, the letters seemed to move or dance on the page. Jessie had always been an excellent reader. Apparently, for dyslexics, reading aloud was like torture. Jessie wanted to feel happy because she could do something so much better than Ian. Instead, she felt sorry for him.

What does Ian do to Julia during the lesson?

How does Mr Jones react to Ian's dyslexia?

Think about it…

The class is studying *The Merchant of Venice* by Shakespeare. Some people think that this play should no longer be studied because of the negative way that Shylock, a Jew, is described. Shakespeare has been accused of anti-Semitism. Others call this attitude "cancel culture". Do you think that we should stop reading literature from the past because we no longer agree with it? Or should we use it as a way to discuss what is right and wrong?

Ian is dyslexic. Do you know someone with dyslexia? What do you know about it?

6 **thick** slang for stupid – 12 **torture** painful punishment

Chapter 8

The next morning, Jessie put on her new crop top. She had made the top from an old t-shirt she had found in the street. It was red with the word "Pow" on the front. In fact, when she found it, the word was "Power", but she had sewn a circle over the "er". It looked cool. Crop tops were not allowed at Jessie's school and were definitely not part of the uniform, but Jessie decided to wear it anyway. Most of the time, the teachers said nothing or didn't notice.

"Whatever *next*!" exclaimed her mother, who was standing up eating an apple.

"Why aren't you sitting down for breakfast?" asked Jessie, saying nothing to her mother's comment.

"I read that if you eat standing up, you put on less weight."

27 **to exclaim** to say loudly in surprise

"Whatever *next*!" laughed Jessie. "Do you think the food drops down to your feet or something? Where do you read this stuff?"

Her mother looked uncomfortable. "I can't remember the science behind it, but, well, it could work, don't you think?" She sounded unsure.

"Anyway, don't you like my top?" And Jessie stood up, held out her arms, and turned around.

"Well, it's… very short."

"That's the fashion, Mum, I thought you liked fashion."

"But it shows your stomach."

"That's the point. I think it looks good. And I made it myself. You should be proud of me, Mum."

"But your stomach is…. not flat, and your skin is so…. white."

"I like it that way. The painter Rubens thought flesh was gorgeous, and I think he was right."

"Rubens?"

"Yes, he was a painter in the 17th century. Very famous."

"Oh…"

"And look at Mary Queen of Scots. She was red haired with a big nose and white skin. Just like me."

"Mary Queen of Scots, eh?"

"Aye!"

Jessie opened the fridge and took out the milk. "I really hate this skimmed milk, Mum. I'll go shopping after school – is there anything else we need? Apart from real milk, I mean?"

Jessie thought her mother was going to say something about low fat, but she seemed to decide against it. Jessie felt like she had won a battle until her mother said suddenly, "I had a call from the school yesterday. I have to go and see your form teacher on Monday. What's her name again?"

Jessie swallowed hard. She felt worried now. "It's Ms Campbell."

1 **to drop** to fall fast – 2 **stuff** things – 12 **proud** feeling of satisfaction or pleasure – 14 **flesh** skin – 24 **skimmed milk** milk with no fat – 28 **battle** fight

"That's right, Mrs Campbell."

"She likes to be called Ms."

"Oh, does she? Well, I hope it will be good news rather than bad news."

Jessie and her mother looked at each other, and they both knew what the other one was thinking. Jessie sipped her watery hot chocolate and said nothing.

What did Jessie do to create her new crop top?

Who called Jessie's mum and asked her to come into school?

Think about it...

Jessie mentions the painter Rubens. In the past it was seen as beautiful to be fat and not thin, but now fashion has changed. What do you think about pressure from society to be a certain shape?

6 **to sip** to drink in small mouthfuls

Chapter 9

That morning, going to school felt easier. Jessie was excited about the poetry club. She had written two more poems and wanted to show them to Mr Jones. It was easy to express feelings in a poem. Talking about problems was more difficult for Jessie. However, as she walked down Prince's Street, she decided to tell Mr Jones about the bullying. Yesterday, Ian was kicking Julia's chair. Clearly, he bullied other people too. Ian had to be stopped. Now Jessie knew that Ian had his own confidence problems, she felt stronger.

Jessie went to the staff room and knocked. Ms Campbell came to open the door. She frowned when she saw Jessie. Was it because of the phone call to her mother? Or because of her crop top?

"Yes?"

---

28 **to knock** to bang on the door

"Good morning, Ms Campbell. I'd like to talk to Mr Jones, please." Jessie knew that it was a good idea to be polite to teachers.

Ms Campbell stared at Jessie's top and for a minute it looked like she was going to say something. Ms Campbell was wearing a tartan skirt and a fair isle jumper, she looked like an advertisement for Scottish clothing.

"I will ask Mr Jones if he has time to see you," said Ms Campbell, and she shut the door in Jessie's face. Jessie did not know what Ms Campbell was going to say to her mother, but perhaps wearing the crop top to school today was a bad idea.

The door opened and Mr Jones stood there, smiling behind his big, dark beard.

"Jessie, perfect timing! I have something to tell you."

"Oh, well… I was wondering if I could tell you something too."

"Absolutely. Let's go into the classroom next door."

They went into the empty classroom and sat down on either side of a desk. Before Jessie could say anything, Mr Jones started talking.

"Your poem was absolutely brilliant, Jessie. You are a natural writer. The words you choose, the way you put them together, it's pure magic. You know, I told you, a well-known poet is coming to give a special performance at the school. His name is Barnaby Brown, I think you will really like his poetry. I'd like to read out your poem at the event. In fact, if you agree, I'd like *you* to read out your poem. What do you think? You could ask your parents to come too."

"Well, it's only my mum…"

"Your mum, then. Perfect. I'm sure she'll be proud of you."

"… Are you sure it's that good, Mr Jones? I mean…."

"Jessie, *believe* in yourself. You have talent! Don't waste it." Usually, Mr Jones was always smiling and joking, but right now he looked very serious.

6 **Fair isle jumper** a Scottish sweater

"Do you think… do you think I could be a writer one day?"

"I think you're *already* a writer! You could be a teacher. You could be all kinds of things. Now, what did you want to talk to me about?"

"Oh, I can't remember now. Nothing important." It suddenly seemed stupid to mention her problems with Ian. Or not the right moment.

Jessie suddenly felt very excited. She could write, and that felt good. But she was scared too. She was going to stand up to say her poem in front of the whole school, especially her mum. Would her mum like it? Would her mum even come? Jessie was not sure.

Why does Jessie go to see Mr Jones in the staff room?

What does Mr Jones talk about instead?

Think about it…

Jessie breaks the rules by wearing a crop top to school. Do you think that students should be allowed to wear crop tops and shorts to school?

What do you think of slam poetry, or poetry in general?

Chapter 10

Saturday mornings were the best time of the week. Jessie liked to sleep for hours and then stay in bed to read her book. Jessie found the book *Trainspotting* in the 'Little Free Library' in Dundas Street. These little libraries were in fact boxes painted in pretty colours and attached to a wall. Anyone could put in a book, or take out a book. No one wanted them any more, and so they were free. Jessie found all of her books in the Little Free Libraries around Edinburgh. Each time, she read the book, then put it back in one of the boxes.

Trainspotting was all about Edinburgh, but it was not the city she knew. The characters were all on drugs and Jessie found the story frightening. But it was well written and she could not put it down. All the words were written with a Scottish accent, just like people speak in Edinburgh. Sentences like "*Ah wis jist sitting*

23 **attached** connected, fixed

thair" meant "I was just sitting there". To start with, it was difficult to read, but soon it became easy. Jessie was fascinated.

Mum had gone to the gym when Jessie finally got out of bed. She was hungry and it was lunchtime, and the cupboard was empty, as usual. Jessie put on a green top and a pair of jeans and went down the road.

Jessie and her mum lived in a tiny flat, but Jessie did not mind because they were right in the centre of the city, on Cowgate Street. This part of Edinburgh was called the 'Old Town' and some of the buildings were medieval. When Jessie walked out the door, there were beautiful old buildings everywhere. The streets were dark and mysterious. She could walk past St Giles' Cathedral up to Edinburgh Castle, and past the Old College and Edinburgh University. She liked the arches and towers and the beautiful old stone, and all the little shops that sold interesting things. On Saturdays, like today, there were groups of tourists on walking tours. She could hear them talking about how beautiful Edinburgh was, and she felt proud of her city.

But it can be cold in Scotland, even in the summer, and Jessie was only wearing a light top. It was a windy day and soon it started to rain. Jessie hurried to the 'New Town', which was next to the 'Old Town'. The buildings in the 'New Town' were in fact quite old, about 250 years old! But they were not as old as the buildings in the 'Old Town'.

Jessie was going to visit her favourite fish and chip shop, L'Alba D'Oro, which had an Italian name but was definitely Scottish. This was the best place to buy fish and chips, but it was cheaper to buy black pudding or haggis or pizza, all deep-fried. Mum did not approve of deep-fried food, but Jessie loved it, especially deep-fried cheese and tomato pizza. However, she did not want to

10 **Medieval** from the Middle Ages (AD 600 to AD 1500) – 12 **mysterious** strange, hard to understand – 14 **arch** a curved structure – 28 **black pudding** blood sausage – 28 **haggis** Scottish dish made from sheep – 28 **deep-fried** fried in a lot of oil

spend too much money today and decided to buy only a portion of chips.

She stood behind the person at the counter. Those shoulders looked very familiar, and she recognised that green jumper. Ian! In her part of town. In the chippy. He was at the front of the queue giving his order.

"I'll have a two fish cakes with chips please."

"Salt 'n' sauce?"

"Mmm, no sauce, *jis* salt and vinegar."

"Aye, you Glaswegians don't like sauce, do you?"

The man had recognised Ian's accent and he was laughing at him. Jessie wondered if Ian was angry, but she could not see his face.

"Large or small chips?"

"Large."

"That's £4.90 plus £5.90 for the fish cakes. That will be £10.80, please. Wait to the side for a couple of minutes, I'll call you when the cakes are fried."

Ian turned around and suddenly Jessie and Ian were face to face.

Jessie froze. Ian froze.

"What's your order, Jessie?" The man called over Ian's head. He knew Jessie because she was a regular customer.

"I'll just have a large portion of chips, please. With salt and sauce, of course."

Jessie had to stand to the side next to Ian. She felt hot and nervous. They did not speak to each other. Jessie looked at her feet.

Their orders arrived at the same time.

"One portion of fish cakes and chips with vinegar and salt, one large chips with sauce and salt. Glasgow meets Edinburgh, eh?" said the chip man. He winked at them. It was embarrassing.

---

5 **chippy** slang for a fish and chip shop – 6 **queue** line of people waiting – 9 **jis** Scottish pronunciation of 'just' – 9 **vinegar** liquid made from wine, eaten with chips in the UK – 21 **to freeze** to stop moving

Jessie turned to walk out the shop when Ian said very quietly, "Those chips look disgusting. White and red, just like you."

She looked up at him and met his angry eyes. Jessie felt angry too. She wanted to be cruel, just like Ian.

"That sauce is brown, not red, stupid! Do you have trouble with colours as well as words?"

She glared at him. This was her town, her chip shop, and her sauce. She walked out the chip shop and onto the street, putting chips into her mouth, but her hand was shaking. *That was a bad thing to say*, she thought, *It's not Ian's fault that he is dyslexic. Still, he is a bully, and he needs to learn a lesson.*

The sun had come out but it was still cold. Jessie walked fast to keep warm. She went in the direction of Arthur's Seat, dipping her chips into the sauce. Slowly, she calmed down. After a while she came to her favourite bookshop. She stopped in front of the window to look at the books. The window was like a mirror in the sunshine. Ian was standing right behind her! Jessie kept walking fast. It was difficult to eat the chips and walk at the same time, but she kept going until she reached Holyrood Park. She almost ran up the hill until she got to Arthur's Seat and sat down, out of breath and hot.

Jessie sat for a long time, looking at Edinburgh. She could see the spires of the churches below and the castle. Jessie was breathing more slowly now. She tried to eat her chips but they were cold.

"Yuk! Your chips look *really* disgusting now!"

She could not believe it – Ian was standing beside her, looking down. Was he going to kick her again? Jessie tried to move, but she was frozen with fear. She was confident in the chip shop, but now, alone on the hill, Ian seemed big, strong and frightening.

In one movement, Ian sat down beside her. What was he going to do? She did not dare to look at him.

---

2 **disgusting** a bad taste or look – 4 **cruel** unkind – 9 **to shake** to move uncontrollably – 10 **fault** responsibility for sth you cannot help – 13 **to dip** to put in and out quickly – 23 **spire** pointed tower of a church

"I..." began Ian. His voice sounded different. "I'm sorry. You look a lot better than that disgusting sauce."

Was this a kind of compliment? Jessie looked at Ian and was surprised to see him smile. He had a nice smile and it changed his face.

"I'm sorry too. I mean... what I said about your reading and the colours. It was not okay. It's not your fault, I know."

"Mmm."

She felt that he was angry again and decided to change the subject.

"The view is amazing from here, isn't it? I love this place. Look, you can see the cathedral and the castle, and the Firth of Forth."

"The what?"

"The Firth of Forth. The Forth is the name of the river, and a firth is an estuary, which is where the river meets the sea."

"Oh." Ian did not seem interested. "It's OK. But Glasgow is better. It's cool and full of music and cool culture. Edinburgh's only full of tourists. It's like a museum. And there are too many hills. You can't skateboard."

Jessie tried not to be angry.

"Skateboard? So why didn't you stay in Glasgow if it's so good?"

"I *didnae* want to come...." That strong Glasgow accent again. Ian seemed to realise and looked embarrassed. He carried on, 'My parents split up. I came here with my dad, he comes *frae* Edinburgh. My mum stayed in Glasgow."

"I see. Sounds like the opposite of my life. My parents split and my dad moved to Glasgow."

"Really? So have you been to Glasgow?"

"*Aye*. I didn't like it. I suppose it isn't home. Home is where your friends are."

"*Aye*, it is. I miss my friends. And skateboarding. I'm not a good reader but I'm a brilliant skateboarder. I used to spend all

---

3 **compliment** positive comment – 22 **didnae** Scottish pronunciation of 'did not'

day at Kelvingrove Skatepark, teaching other kids sometimes. Glasgow is brilliant for skateboarding. It's the best."

"You can skateboard in Edinburgh too, Ian. Sometimes I go to Saughton Skate Park and watch the skaters. Some of them are really good."

"You should see me skateboard." Ian sounded very confident again. Too confident.

"Well… you could go and see. Maybe you could show them what you can do."

"The trouble is, I had to leave Glasgow quickly and I forgot my skateboard. I *cannae* believe it. Do you know where I can buy a skateboard here? Or do you only know where the bookshops are?" He was smiling. Just a bit, but he was smiling.

"You know, you look much nicer when you smile."

Ian's eyes went dark again.

"There's a skateboard shop in Canongate," said Jessie. "Do you want me to show you?"

"I *didnae* mean I wanted *tae* go with you!" he shouted. He was making his Glasgow accent stronger. "I'll find it *maeself*."

He was gone. One minute he was angry, the next minute he was not. Jessie looked at the Firth of Forth and finished her cold chips. Ian had problems, that was clear. She was shivering and it was time to go home and manage her own problems.

Where do Jessie and her Mum live?

How does the man in the chip shop know that Ian is from Glasgow?

11 **cannae** Scottish pronunciation of 'cannot' – 18 **didnae** Scottish pronunciation of 'did not' – 18 **tae** Scottish pronunciation of 'to' – 19 **maeself** Scottish pronunciation of 'myself' – 22 **to shiver** to shake with the cold

Think about it…

In Scotland, many people like to eat deep-fried food including chips with different sauces. Do you think you would like to eat the kinds of food they eat in Scotland? How do you like your chips?

Jessie is worried that Ian will kick her, although he doesn't. Do you think physical violence is worse than verbal violence?

Chapter 11

Jessie did the shopping. She used the twenty pounds that her mum had left. She tidied the kitchen and noticed that the floor was covered in crumbs, so she swept it. Then she realised that the floor was dirty, so she washed it with a floor cloth.

The kitchen looked really clean and Jessie felt satisfied. Was Mum going to be pleased? Perhaps she could make dinner too? Her mother was much later than usual. Jessie put some water to boil to make pasta and chopped up onions to make a tomato sauce. She heard the door open and her mother's footsteps, which were fast and angry.

Her mother arrived in the kitchen like a storm. "You really are in trouble, aren't you?" she hissed. "I've just been with that Mrs Campbell. She told me you don't go to school every day. Your

20 **to tidy** to put everything in its place – 21 **crumb** small piece, often of food – 30 **to hiss** to make a noise like a snake

end-of-year grades will be terrible. You will go nowhere in life. Do you really want to be a *loser*?"

She looked grey and tired and clearly did not expect Jessie to reply. In fact, she had already left the room. The kitchen filled with the smell of burned onions. Her mother had not noticed how clean it all was.

Jessie wondered if she should go and tell her mum about the poetry evening, but it did not seem like the right moment. Perhaps she would be proud of her and see that she had some kind of future? Probably, though, she would not be impressed. After all, she was not impressed with Jessie's sewing. Her mum wanted her to get a safe, boring job like an accountant or a nurse. A doctor would be even better. She wasn't interested in creation. Or even books.

Jessie wanted her mother to understand her. She felt angry. So angry that she kicked the kitchen chair. *I'm like Weegie Ian the bully*, she thought. *He's in a place he does not want to be. And he's dyslexic too. No wonder he's so horrible to everyone. He is angry and frustrated and that's why he is so aggressive.*

Jessie decided to be less angry. She did not want to be like Ian after all. She must find a way to get Mum to come to the poetry reading. She wanted her mother to be proud of her.

The next day, Mum was not at the breakfast table. She had gone to work already. Jessie ate an apple for breakfast. She thought her mother would be pleased. But then she felt hungry all morning.

2 **loser** sb who does badly – 12 **boring** not exciting at all – 12 **accountant** sb who works with numbers and money

Why is Jessie's mum so angry?

Why doesn't Jessie tell her mum about the poetry evening?

Think about it ...

Jessie's mum wants her to do a "safe, boring job" so that she won't be a "loser". Do you think that is a typical parent reaction?

Many parents today say they don't understand their children because they live in such a different world (phones, social media, video games, etc.). Do you think that the gap is too big?

Chapter 12

When Jessie arrived at the school gates, her head was full of a new poem about a woman in a painting by Rubens. The words came as she walked along and she needed to write them down. She had no pen or paper, so she took out her phone and decided to write her ideas as notes.

"Put that phone away now!" She looked up and saw the deputy head frowning at her. Of course, you were not allowed to use mobile phones inside school. Oh, no, in trouble again! Jessie quickly put the phone in her pocket, smiled politely and went to her first lesson, which was English. Jessie felt good about her English lesson today and walked confidently into the classroom.

Mr Jones told them to open *The Merchant of Venice*. Jessie wondered where Ian was sitting this morning, and turned round to look at the classroom. He was not there.

At the end of the lesson, Mr Jones said that he had an announcement to make.

"After school, Barnaby Brown is coming to perform in the main hall. He's a great poet and I think you will all enjoy his poetry reading. One of your classmates has been chosen to read her own poem. I invite you all to come along and find out who it is!" Mr Jones walked out the room.

"I bet it's Jessie!" the boy in front of her said to his neighbour.

"In any case, I think I'll go. It sounds fun. Barnaby Brown is a fantastic slam poet, I saw him once on TV."

"OK. I've never heard of him, but I'm interested."

"Imagine reading your poem after Barnaby Brown. That's impressive."

"*Aye*, let's go and find out who it is."

Jessie felt nervous and excited. She needed to practise reading her poem. She decided to go to her special place under the trees and rehearse.

When she got there, she was surprised to see a tall, dark shape near her tree. She immediately recognised Ian. Perhaps he was waiting for her. She was not sure if he was going to be a bully or a friend this morning. Jessie was not nervous. She went towards the trees and stood beside Ian. He looked up suddenly. He seemed surprised. She was expecting him to say something like, "You look ugly in that t-shirt". But Jessie felt confident because she had been chosen to read her poem with Barnaby Brown.

"Hi, ginger!" said Ian quietly. Instead of feeling bad, Jessie laughed.

"Hi, blockhead!" she replied. She noticed that Ian flinched. She felt mean. Ian was not stupid, after all, he simply had dyslexia. Calling people names was not a solution.

"I take that back. I'm sorry," she said quickly.

3 **classmate** sb in the same class – 15 **to rehearse** to practise for a performance – 17 **shape** form – 27 **blockhead** a stupid person – 27 **to flinch** to make a quick, nervous movement

Ian stood up. He was much bigger than her and Jessie wondered if he was going to kick her. She felt scared, but she kept on talking.

"Lots of people are dyslexic. It's no big deal. It doesn't mean you are stupid and I should not have called you a blockhead."

Ian was looking at her very hard. He was trying to control his anger. He looked like he was going to explode. He did not hit her, or say anything. He simply walked away.

Jessie sighed with relief. She realised that she was trembling. *I will not let him upset me*, she said to herself. *Anyway, time to practise reading my poem.*

What announcement does Mr Jones make during the English lesson?

Why does Jessie feel more confident in front of Ian now?

Think about it...

Do you think you should be able to use mobile phones at school? What are the advantages and disadvantages?

Jessie thinks that calling people names is not a solution, but she still does it. Do you think she is bullying Ian?

7 **to explode** to burst violently

Chapter 13

The school hall was crowded. Jessie felt very nervous because she was going to read her poem in front of so many people. That morning, she had sent her mum a text:

She did not say that she had written the poem herself, or explain that Barnaby Brown was coming. But she did not think her mother would come anyway, straight after work. Perhaps it was best if she did not.

Some of the poetry group members were standing with Jessie.

"You're going to be brilliant," said Siri, squeezing her arm.

"Yes, I really admire you. You have been chosen to read a poem after Barnaby Brown – that's *braw*!" Elliot smiled at Jessie. He

30 **to squeeze** to press firmly – 32 **braw** Scottish for 'great'

really did seem to admire her. Jessie felt warm and scared at the same time.

Barnaby Brown came onto the stage and everyone clapped. He started to perform some of his poems, which were about inequality and race. He jumped around and threw his arms into the air. He spoke and sang and made signs at the audience. He invited people to answer the questions in his poems. He was brilliant. Jessie felt inspired and excited by what he said. She almost forgot that it was nearly her turn.

"And now," said Barnaby, "I would like to hear some of your poetry. Alan Jones has told me about his poetry club. He says that some of you get together and talk about poetry, and write your own poems, and I think that is absolutely amazing! He has chosen one of those pupils to read her poem to us tonight. And I'm really looking forward to hearing it. I would like to invite Jessie Redford up onto the stage. Give her a big round of applause everyone, please!"

And the whole room started clapping and cheering. Jessie felt her legs shaking and her heart beating very hard. She was not sure if she could get up onto the stage to read her poem. But Zara gave her a gentle push forward, and Siri said, "You can do it, Jessie, you can do it!" And so she walked up the steps onto the stage and looked down at the full room and took a deep breath.

The poem had a life of its own. Jessie did not have to think. The words flowed out of her like a river. As she finished it, she finally saw the audience was looking at her. And Mum was standing right at the back. She must have arrived late. Her face was all red and shining with tears.

After the reading, Barnaby Brown returned to the stage and joined in the applause. He had a great big smile on his face and he was shaking his head. "I can't believe it!" he cried out when the clapping had stopped. "Jessie, that was amazing. You have got

13 **to look forward to sth** to want sth to happen – 14 **round of applause** clapping (to tap your hands in approval). – 16 **to clap** to tap your hands in approval – 16 **to cheer** to shout to encourage or approve – 23 **to flow** to move like liquid

talent!" And everyone started clapping again. "Are your mum and dad here tonight, Jessie?" asked Barnaby.

"Just my mum."

"Jessie's mum, can you hold up your hand, please!" called out Barnaby. He was such a performer. Everyone looked round as Jessie's mum raised her hand. "Well, Mrs Redford, you must be a very proud Mum, right?" said Barnaby, and the whole audience watched Jessie's mother nodding her head. She was crying so hard she found it difficult to say anything.

Later, everyone came to congratulate Jessie.

"I could really feel the loneliness in the poem," said Bella.

"Yes, I love the comparison with the bird." "It was beautiful." "Your poem made me sad. It really moved me."

At last, Jessie saw her mum talking to Mr Jones and Ms Campbell. As she got near, they stopped speaking and looked at her.

Ms Campbell was the first to speak. "I was telling your mother that you have missed a lot of your lessons lately."

The balloon burst, and Jessie felt her excitement disappear. Ms Campbell was looking at her crop top and frowning. Mr Jones said nothing, but he was smiling as usual.

"I know Jessie has been missing school," said Mum unexpectedly. "But she was writing, you see. And sewing. That top she is wearing: she made it herself, from an old t-shirt. She has this amazing creative mind. Like Shakespeare. Or Rubens."

Her mum stood there looking very serious. Ms Campbell's mouth was open, she clearly did not know what to say. Jessie felt happiness flow through her like water. Mr Jones decided to change the subject.

"Violet," he said to Ms Campbell (so that was her first name!), "I need to talk to you about a pupil in your class. He has dyslexia but it wasn't in his records. Can we go and have a chat…?"

---

19 **to burst** to break suddenly – 32 **record** written information about sth

"Mr Jones, before you go..." began Jessie, and he turned around in surprise.

"Yes, Jessie?"

"I know you mean Ian. I have to talk to you about him. I have an idea."

What are Barnaby Brown's poems about?

How does Jessie's mum react after the poetry reading?

Think about it...

Jessie's mum is proud of her daughter when she sees her read her poem on stage, but not everyone is as talented as Jessie. Would you have reacted the same, do you think?

Do you think Jessie should be punished for missing school? Or is it now okay because she has written a successful poem and proved that she has talent?

Chapter 14

The next morning, Jessie got up at 6 am! Mum was in the kitchen cooking porridge.

"You're up very early," she said. Her voice was bright and she was smiling.

"Yes, I wanted to go and check something before school."

"What do you have to check? Where are you going?" asked Mum. This was new. Normally, her mother was not interested in Jessie's day.

"Um… well, it's a skateboard park."

"A *skateboard* park? Do you like skateboarding now?"

"No. It's for someone else."

"You are full of surprises, Jessie. You know, I realise that we don't talk very much about your life. About what you are doing. I was… well, I was really proud of you last night. You have such talent. Not just the poem you wrote, but the way you said it. I was impressed. Everyone was. And your sewing. I admit that I don't always like what you make, but I can see that you have talent. A lot of talent…."

Jessie felt embarrassed. Mum never said things like this. She did not know what to say.

"Um, thanks Mum."

Her mother put the porridge on the table. She could see the brown sugar on top.

"Did you make porridge with sugar?"

"Yes, and milk. I decided to let you be who you are! I like it with water and salt, you like it with milk and sugar. And that's okay!"

Jessie laughed, and Mum laughed. Jessie stood up and gave her mum a big hug. Which felt good.

It took nearly half an hour to get to Saughton Skate Park. It was only half past seven, but two teenagers were already skating. They went very fast and did amazing jumps and spins. Jessie was impressed. She was scared to talk to them, but she remembered going on stage to say her poem. She took a deep breath and went up to one of the boys.

"Excuse me, can I ask you something?"

Why does Jessie get up so early?

What does Jessie's mum do to show that she is pleased with her?

13 **to hug** to hold sb in your arms – 16 **to spin** to turn around quickly

Think about it...

Jessie's mum seems to forgive her for everything. Do you think she will now accept her daughter completely, or is life not so simple?

Do you think skateboarding is cool, or is it dangerous? What sport do you like best?

Chapter 15

Jessie was late for school, but the deputy headmaster, who was at the gate, simply smiled.

"Good morning, Jessie," he said. "I thought you were brilliant last night."

Jessie immediately felt like a star! Everyone wanted to talk to her. Some people asked about her writing, and said that they loved her poem and the way she read it. A lot of them were interested in her crop top and wanted to order one.

It was all very exciting, but at breaktime, Jessie was exhausted. She wanted to be alone for a minute and think about everything. She decided to go and read her book quietly under the trees. She immediately saw Ian, which was annoying. But perhaps this was the right moment. She needed to talk to him.

"Hey, Ian!"

27 **exhausted** very tired – 30 **annoying** irritating, sth you do not want

"Hi, Jessie. I was waiting for you."

"I don't really care if you think my hair is ugly. Or my nose. I like the way I am." Jessie was not sure if she really meant that, but saying it felt fantastic!

"You looked pretty good last night when you read your poem. I was really impressed."

This was unexpected. Jessie did not know what to say, so instead she sat down next to Ian.

"I didn't know you were there. Well, thanks. I wanted to tell you that I went to a skateboard park this morning."

"What?"

"I went to Saughton skateboard park and I spoke to some skateboarders. They have this club that meets every Saturday afternoon. They do competitions. I spoke to them about you."

"Why do you care?"

"I don't know really. Maybe I wanted to show you that Edinburgh is as good as Glasgow. But it's true that Glasgow is better for skateboarding. That's what these boys told me. They said the skateboarding scene in Glasgow was brilliant. They want to meet you. But you will need a skateboard of course."

"I already bought a skateboard. Thanks for telling me about the shop. But, I don't understand why you did that – why you went to the skateboard park for me."

Ian sounded a bit angry. And also a bit pleased.

"Ian, this is going to sound weird…"

He turned to look at her with his amazing green eyes. He really was good looking, and she did not feel scared of him at all any more. He was waiting for her to continue. Jessie took a deep breath. This was harder than reading her poem in front of the whole school.

"I'd like to help you with your reading. I know it sounds funny. Maybe it makes you feel a bit uncomfortable. But I taught both of

---

25 **weird** strange, unusual

my cousins to read, and one of them has dyslexia. I really enjoyed it. In fact… I think I was good at it. Teaching I mean."

"Another Jessie talent."

Was Ian being sarcastic? She looked at him hard. Was he angry?

"I talked to Mr Jones about it."

"To Mr *Jones*?" Now Ian really did seem ready to walk away.

"Yes, don't worry. Mr Jones is a fantastic teacher, very supportive. He said it was a good idea and that if you wanted to, we could sit next to each other in class and I could help you with extra lessons if necessary."

"Extra lessons? Why would you do that?"

"I suppose it makes me feel good. Useful."

Ian was not smiling. Jessie saw that familiar anger in his eyes. But then it passed like a cloud moving over the sun.

"OK, ginger minger, I agree!"

"That's great, Ian, but no name calling. Otherwise I'll call you a blockhead. But you're not a blockhead, you have simply got dyslexia. Like lots of people."

Ian nodded slowly. "And you have simply got ginger hair. You look like a Scottish queen," he said, and held out his hand.

"Shake on it?"

"Shake on it," said Jessie. She had never felt so good.

Why does Jessie feel like a star at school?

Why do the boys at the skateboard park want to meet Ian?

4 **sarcastic** saying the opposite of what you mean to laugh at so – 22 **to shake on sth** to shake hands to agree on sth

Think about it...

Do you think that Jessie did the right thing to talk to the skateboarders? Can you imagine taking a risk like that?

In the end, Jessie offers to be a “buddy” to Ian and help him with his English. Do you think that having someone your own age help you at school could be a good way to make progress?

Activities

Focus on the story

1. What happened and when?

1. Fill in the missing words. You can look back at the story. Every Edinburgh schoolchild knows that the ____________ is actually longer than a mile and that kings and queens used to cross it.

2. Jessie made her way to ______ Hill and climbed up to the ________ Monument, which looks like an unfinished Greek __________.

3. Jessie could see Edinburgh __________ and the Balmoral _________ Tower, with the river in the distance.

4. Her father had taken her to the ______________ Tea Rooms designed by Rennie _____________.

5. But Glasgow did not have anything like the Palace of _______________ or Edinburgh Castle, or the amazing views.

6. The _____________ is the name of the river, and a firth is an estuary, which is where the river meets the sea.

2. True or false?

Tick the correct box.

		True	False
1.	In *The Merchant of Venice*, Shylock is a Jewish money lender.	☐	☐
2.	In Edinburgh, local people like to eat their chips with salt and sauce.	☐	☐
3.	Scottish people traditionally make porridge with milk and sugar.	☐	☐

		True	False
4.	The Old Town in Edinburgh has medieval buildings.	☐	☐
5.	The New Town in Edinburgh has Art Deco buildings.	☐	☐
6.	Rubens was a French painter during the 17th century.	☐	☐
7.	Mary Queen of Scots had red hair.	☐	☐
8.	In Scottish chip shops, you can buy deep-fried pizza.	☐	☐
9.	*Trainspotting* is a novel set in Glasgow.	☐	☐
10.	Edinburgh is very popular with tourists, but no one visits Glasgow.	☐	☐
11.	The Royal Mile measures exactly one mile.	☐	☐

Focus on the people

1. What do you know about them?

	 Jessie	 Ian
lives in…		
likes…		
doesn't like…		
personal challenges…		

2. True or false?

Tick the correct box.

		True	False
1.	Jessie likes making new clothes out of old clothes.	☐	☐
2.	Jessie's school uniform is a tartan skirt, a blue jumper and a tie.	☐	☐
3.	Jessie has straight red hair.	☐	☐
4.	Ian was born in Edinburgh and then moved to Glasgow.	☐	☐
5.	Ian misses Glasgow because he used to be a successful skateboarder in the city.	☐	☐
6.	The English teacher Mr Jones has a bald head, a dark beard and glasses.	☐	☐
7.	Jessie's form teacher is called Mrs McGonagall.	☐	☐
8.	Zara, Siri and Elliot are in the same class as Jessie and Ian.	☐	☐

3. Friends or enemies?

Jessie is from Edinburgh and Ian is from Glasgow, which are very different towns. They have different accents and eat their chips in a different way! What else is different about them?
Which adjectives do you think describe them best?

shy	aggressive	confident	talented	attractive
impolite	happy	sad	open-minded	judgemental

Jessie	
Ian	

Focus on grammar

1. What's the missing preposition?

Look at Chapter 2. Put the right preposition with the verb.

1. Most of the students carried __ talking to each other.
2. A tall, slim boy stood ____.
3. He had a long scar _____ his left cheek.
4. Jessie was thinking _______ how she could transform a check shirt into a bag.
5. The tapping ____ the chair continued.
6. Most of Jessie's friends were bent _______ their screens.
7. Your phone was supposed to be turned _____ during the day.
8. She was leaning _______ a tree trunk.
9. He suddenly bent ________ and whispered in her ear.
10. Jessie put ________ her book and saw the title was blurred.

2. What's the correct verb form?

Fill in the following verbs in the correct form.

1. In fact, when she found it, the word was "Power", but she had __________ (to sew) a circle over the "er".
2. I already __________ (to buy) a skateboard. Thanks for telling me about the shop.
3. Mr Jones ___________ (to come) in the room and started the lesson.
4. He ___________ (to tell) them about characters and metaphors and about listening to your thoughts.
5. Jessie _______ (to shut) her book and looked up.
6. She _________ (to think) they would all be slim and attractive.
7. Jessie ________ (to sip) her watery hot chocolate and said nothing.
8. She had _______________ (to write) two more poems and wanted to show them to Mr Jones.

3. Which preposition goes where?

The prepositions are all mixed up. Put them in the right place.

1. Why aren't you sitting on for breakfast?
2. I read that if you eat standing down, you put out less weight.
3. Do you think the food drops up to your feet or something?
4. And Jessie stood around, held against her arms, and turned up.
5. .... but she seemed to decide down it.
6. She almost ran off the hill until she got to Arthur's Seat.
7. Of course, nobody turned up their phone.

Build your vocabulary

Focus on words and phrases

1. What does the word mean?

Match the words on the left with the definitions on the right.

1	porridge	a	Scottish dish made from a sheep's stomach
2	tartan	b	Scottish for 'yes'
3	piper	c	from Glasgow
4	kilt	d	a Scottish sweater
5	Weegie	e	a patterned Scottish cloth
6	Glaswegian	f	someone from Scotland
7	Scot	g	someone who plays Scottish bagpipes
8	Aye	h	slang for someone from Glasgow
9	Fair isle jumper	i	a Scottish skirt for men
10	haggis	j	a typical Scottish breakfast of oats boiled in water or milk

1	2	3	4	5	6	7	8	9	10
j									

2. What's the word?

The words below are mixed up. Write the correct version in the box.

ppingski		gredoan	
cycledup		rancig	
spscri		turetor	
roobetet		kcknoed	
atfol		vershiign	

3. What do you think the following words mean?

1 to wave	a to move your hand as a signal b to smile at someone c to hit with the foot	6 to hiss	a to make a noise like a snake b to make a noise like a bird c to make a noise like a lion
2 to join in	a to make two things into one b to do sth together c to eat your dinner	7 exhausted	a very big b very tired c very easy
3 a flash	a a sudden feeling b a skirt for Scottish men c a sharp pain	8 weird	a strange, unusual b slow c fashionable
4 to hang out	a to eat very fast b to write c to spend time with	9 to care	a to drive a car b to feel concern or interest c to eat fast
5 bald	a with no teeth b with no fingers c with no hair	10 busy	a full of people b empty c heavy

Glasgow Meets Edinburgh – the mind map

Make your own mind map words connected to the story. Think of words to add to each topic area. You can add your own topic areas too.

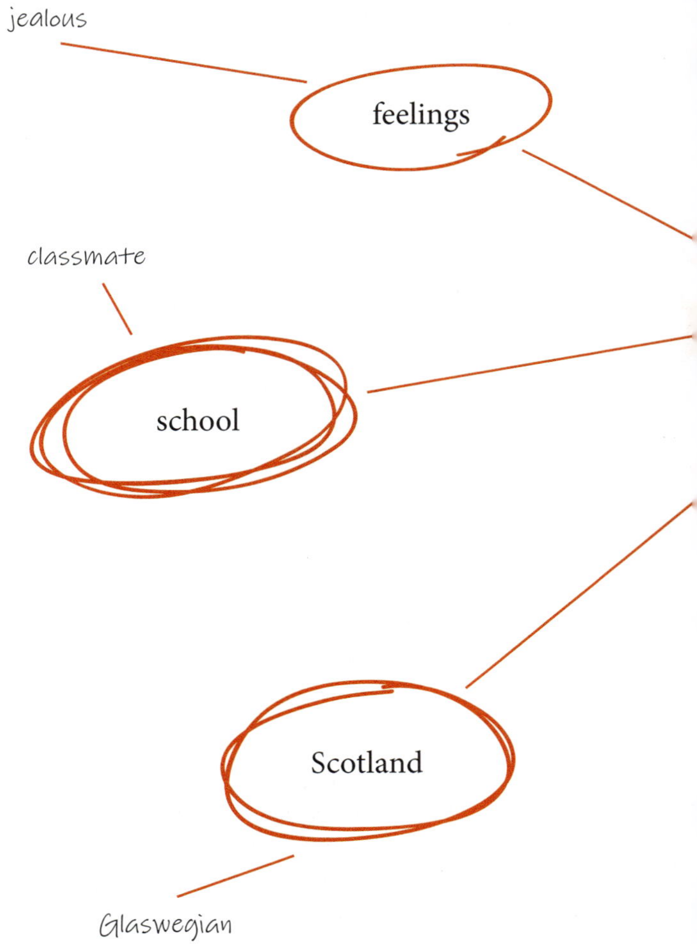

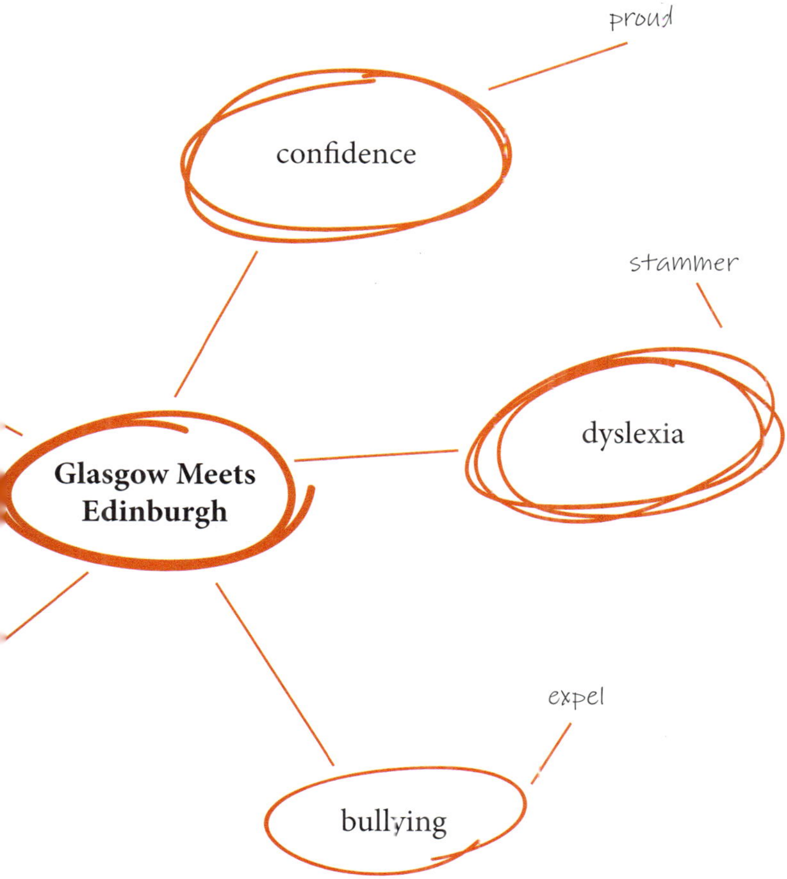

Compare your words with the words on the next pages. Did you include some of the same words? Tick the words you know and look back at the text and explanations to check the meanings of any new words. You can add your own words and notes to the glossary like the examples.

Glossary

	New word?	Notes / connected words
Scotland		
Fair isle	☐	
Glaswegian	☐	
haggis	☐	
kilt	☐	
piper	☐	
porridge	☐	
Scot	☐	
tartan	☐	
Bullying		
cruel	☐	
expel	☐	
flinch	☐	
glare	☐	
hiss	☐	
kick	☐	
rivalry	☐	
stare	☐	
toxic	☐	
victim	☐	
Dyslexia		
encourage	☐	
(feeling like a) loser	☐	
open-minded	☐	
panic	☐	
reading	☐	
stammer	☐	
torture	☐	

	New word?	Notes / connected words
Confidence		
cheer	☐	
compliment	☐	
deal with	☐	
hug	☐	
impressed	☐	
join in	☐	
look forward to	☐	
proud	☐	
round of applause	☐	
sort out	☐	
talent	☐	
Feelings		
absorbed	☐	
annoying	☐	
boring	☐	
disgust	☐	
exhausted	☐	
fed up	☐	
hatred	☐	
inspired	☐	
jealous	☐	
School		
classmate	☐	
corridor	☐	
expel	☐	
form teacher	☐	
get into trouble	☐	
rehearse	☐	
skip lessons	☐	

Find out more

1. Glasgow

The story describes most of the monuments in Edinburgh. What are the tourist attractions in the city of Glasgow? Which one would you like to visit? Why?

2. Scotland in the United Kingdom

Scotland is part of the United Kingdom. However, many Scots would like to see Scotland become an independent country. There have been three important referendums in Scotland – in 1979, 1997 and 2014. What were they about and what new powers were given to Scotland?

Try and find out the following information.

Size of Scotland: ______ km² Size of the UK: ______ km²

Population of Scotland: ______ million
Population of the UK: ______ million

Does Scotland have its own parliament?

Does Scotland have its own leader? If so, what is his/her name?

Is Scottish money the same as in the rest of the UK?

What is the Scottish language called and how many people use it?

3. Dyslexia

Dyslexia affects 10% of the British population, which means that it is very common. You probably have a friend with dyslexia or maybe you are dyslexic. What support does your school provide to help dyslexic people? See if you can find out whether it allows dyslexic students:

- more time to finish their work
- more time to do exams
- the possibility to use a computer or tablet in class
- the possibility to use a computer or tablet in exams
- extra support lessons
- extra support material
- the possibility to work with another, non-dyslexic student

Work together in a small group. Create a proposal for how you could make your school more dyslexia-friendly? Use the internet for your research. Think about, for example, your class, your teachers, the learning tools and materials in the school, and the school itself.

Present your ideas to the class or write a proposal to send to your school principal.

Answer key

Before you start

1	2	3	4	5	6
c	a	d	f	b	e

Suggested answers. Students should think of their own and share their ideas.

country	Scotland	Northern Ireland	England	Wales
cities	Edinburgh, Glasgow, Aberdeen	Belfast, Londonderry, Armagh	Nottingham, Manchester, London	Cardiff, Wrexham, Swansea
flag colours	dark blue with diagonal white cross	white background with diagonal red cross	white background with horizontal / vertical red cross	red / green / white
symbols	thistle	shamrock	red rose, three lions	leek / daffodil
famous things	Nessie	"The Troubles"	The Royal Family	castles
Famous people	Andy Murray, Gordon Ramsay	Rory McIlroy, Liam Neeson	Harry Styles, Harry Kane	Catherine Zeta Jones, Gareth Bale

Questions at the end of each chapter

Chapter 1

- with milk and sugar
- Princess Street, Edinburgh Castle, North Bridge, Royal Mile and St Giles Cathedral

Chapter 2

- because of his accent
- behind a tree in the corner of the school yard

Chapter 3

- The National Monument
- because she loves writing poetry and Mr Jones tells here that she is a good writer

Chapter 4

- Margie and Bella
- He is tall with green eyes and he wears expensive clothes

Chapter 5

- *Trainspotting* by Irvine Welsh
- She think her upcycled skirt is amazing and wants to order one.

Chapter 6

- Rubens
- Mary Queen of Scots

Chapter 7

- He kicks the back of her chair.
- He tells him to come and see him after class to organise some support.

Chapter 8

- She took an old t-shirt and sewed a circle on to make the word 'Pow'.
- Mrs Campbell, her form teacher

Chapter 9

- She wants to tell him about Ian and the bullying.
- He tells her about the poetry event and asks her to read her poem.

Chapter 10

- in a tiny flat in the centre of the 'old town'
- from his accent and the way he takes his chips (with vinegar and no sauce)

Chapter 11

- because Mrs Campbell has told her that Jessie has been missing school
- because she thinks that she won't be impressed and it doesn't feel like the right moment

Chapter 12

- Barnaby Brown is coming to perform at the school, and one of the pupils has been chosen to read a poem.
- because she has been chosen to read her poem with Barnaby Brown

Chapter 13

- inequality and race
- She is crying so hard she finds it difficult to speak.

Chapter 14

- to go to the skatepark before school starts
- She makes her porridge with milk and sugar, the way she likes it.

Chapter 15

- because everyone wants to ask her about her poem
- because they think the skateboarding scene in Glasgow is brilliant

Focus on the story

1 1 Royal Mile, 2 Calton Hill, National Monument, Greek temple, 3 Edinburgh Castle, Balmoral Clock Tower, 4 Willow Tea Rooms, Rennie Macintosh, 5 Holyroodhouse, 6 Firth of Forth

2 1 T, 2 T, 3 F, 4 T, 5 F, 6 F, 7 T, 8 T, 9 F, 10 F, 11 F

Focus on the people

1 Students' own answers

2 1 T, 2 F, 3 F, 4 F, 5 T, 6 T, 7 F, 8 F

3 Suggested answers

Jessie	shy talented happy open-minded
Ian	aggressive confident attractive impolite judgemental

Focus on the grammar

1 1 on, 2 up, 3 on, 4 about, 5 on, 6 over, 7 off, 8 against, 9 down, 10 down

2 1 sewn, 2 bought, 3 came, 4 told, 5 shut, 6 thought, 7 sipped, 8 written

3 1 down, 2 up, on, 3 down, 4 up, out, around, 5 against, 6 up, 7 off

Build your vocabulary

1

1	2	3	4	5	6	7	8	9	10
j	e	g	i	h	c	f	b	d	a

2 1 skipping, 2 upcycled, 3 crisps, 4 beetroot, 5 float, 6 groaned, 7 racing, 8 torture, 9 knocked, 10 shivering

3 1 a, 2 b, 3 a, 4 c, 5, c, 6 a, 7 b, 8a, 9b, 10 a

Now do the quizzes!